Life Balloon

Life Balloon

David P. Wrobel

iUniverse, Inc.
New York Lincoln Shanghai

Life Balloon

All Rights Reserved © 2004 by David P. Wrobel

No part of this book may be reproduced or transmitted in any form or by any means, graphic, electronic, or mechanical, including photocopying, recording, taping, or by any information storage retrieval system, without the written permission of the publisher.

iUniverse, Inc.

For information address:
iUniverse, Inc.
2021 Pine Lake Road, Suite 100
Lincoln, NE 68512
www.iuniverse.com

ISBN: 0-595-30959-3 (pbk)
ISBN: 0-595-66225-0 (cloth)

Printed in the United States of America

Dedicated to my wife, my children, my parents, my family, and my partners, thank you for believing in me!

Contents

Preface xi
Using This Book. xiii
CHAPTER 1   Your Life Balloon 1
CHAPTER 2   Have a Great Attitude! 7
CHAPTER 3   GoodFinding. 18
CHAPTER 4   Relationships. 28
CHAPTER 5   Self-Talk 36
CHAPTER 6   Problem Solving 43
CHAPTER 7   Goals. 50
CHAPTER 8   Partners, Mentors, and Coaches 66
Conclusion 71

Preface

Everybody seems to be searching for or writing books on how to have a fulfilled, satisfying life. I spent nine years in door-to-door sales (seeing one hundred people per day) and built a company from two partners to more than five hundred employees and $15 million in annual sales. Along the way I learned a lot and I had the opportunity to put everything I learned into practice building a satisfying life.

I didn't find all the answers, but I did develop a simple analogy (life as a hot-air balloon) that is clear and honest. My hope is that you will use this analogy and this book to find clarity in your life and get a good handle on how to deal with life's challenges.

This book is not a philosophy text; it's a how-to manual. The skills and techniques I've developed from my experiences are broken down into clear, thought-provoking worksheets you can use in your quest.

I learned the things in this book the hard way, through my own actions and reactions. Some insights came from reading and listening to mentors along the way, but I've done all this work and test-driven each technique in my own life. Nothing I'm going to share is a secret; some ideas may even sound familiar. However, the Life Balloon process is more than just ideas; it's a concrete method you can follow to make your own life soar.

I can't begin to tell you how my life has changed since learning the simple skills I will share with you. If this book helps even one person soar, it will be well worth the time it took to write.

Here goes.

Using This Book

You can use this book in a number of ways. So, read this short introduction and then plan your own approach.

Each of the eight chapters introduces a concept, skill, or technique you'll use on your quest for clarity in your life. You'll find plenty of concrete, real-life examples to help you understand the main points of each chapter. Then there are worksheets or exercises to help you put the ideas you learned into practice. The chapters end with some thoughts that will help you carry your new knowledge forward into your own life.

Obviously you'll get more out of this book if you take the time to do each of the exercises thoughtfully and completely. The process of reinventing your life with less stress and more competencies takes some time. Give yourself as long as you need to work through each chapter and absorb what you're learning. Also feel free to make copies of the worksheets if you want to repeat the exercises.

You can use this book on your own, but you might also want to work through it with a partner, mentor, or coach. If you decide to work on it with other people, be sure to set some ground rules about privacy and confidentiality before you begin. This process works best when you are honest and face the hard things squarely. You won't be able to do that if you're worried that your partner is going to tell other people what you've discovered. Write a short statement pledging to maintain confidentiality and then review it periodically as you work.

I wish each of you the best of luck on your journey!

| Self-Education | Charity | Good Relationships | Love |
| Selflessness | Great Attitude | Hope | Kindness | Peace | Persistence | Good Finding |

The HOT AIR- is represented by the GOOD things in our life that make our Life Balloon SOAR!

Four Pieces that make up the **FABRIC** of the balloon are represented by the following characteristics:
1. Values
2. Character
3. Integrity
4. Morals

The **BASKET**- that carries us on our journey is shaped by four sides and the bottom:
1. Family
2. Friends
3. Mentor/Partner
4. Coach

Bottom- *Faith and Beliefs.*

The **SAND BAGS** -- are represented by the negative things in our life that pull our life balloon down preventing us from soaring!
Bad Attitude/Cynicism   Selfishness   Ignorance   Greed   Turmoil   Complaining   Bad Relationships   Hate

1

Your Life Balloon

Have you ever seen a hot-air balloon soaring through the sky completely free and beautiful? Have you ever gone up in a balloon and felt the peace of a ride above the trees and power lines? Floating in the sky it's as if time stops and problems don't exist. What if you could learn to live your life on that more peaceful, obstacle-free plane?

Using this book, you'll imagine your life (business and personal) as a hot-air balloon with four key parts

- The *balloon fabric* is crafted from four segments: character, morals, values, and integrity.

- The *air* that makes the balloon soar is the good things in your life such as hope, peace, love, good relationships, selflessness, a great attitude, and lifelong education. (The more good things in your life, the higher your balloon soars.)

- The *balloon basket* has four sides and a bottom. The sides, which enclose you, are family, friends, mentors/partners, and a coach. The bottom, which supports you, is your faith and beliefs.

- *Sandbags* hanging from the sides are the negative things that pull your life balloon down and prevent it from soaring! Sandbags can be things such as a bad attitude/cynicism, selfishness, greed, turmoil, bad relationships, bad environments, complaining, ignorance, or hate. The more sandbags you carry, the more likely you'll be skidding across the fields of life, hitting the trees and power lines. (You might even be grounded entirely.) Where do sandbags come from?

They might be left over from childhood, or you might have picked them up throughout your life without recognizing them as the baggage they are. You don't need to carry them anymore. You have the right to dump them out of your basket and soar!

You can make a decision to fill your balloon with good things and leave the sandbags behind. The more you focus on developing the good things, the quicker the sandbags will disappear. Concentrating on good things strengthens the fabric of your balloon (your life).

Once you can soar high above the trees and power lines (challenges in your life), you'll see problems more clearly, and with support from a strong balloon and sturdy basket, you'll overcome them more easily.

◆ ◆ ◆

CHAPTER 1 EXERCISE 1

For this exercise you'll use Worksheet 1.

Time to work! First, create a mental picture of what *your* life balloon looks like. What color is it? What condition is the fabric in? How big is the basket? What sandbags are pulling you down?

Next, get a pencil and fill in Worksheet 1 on the following page.

1. Think honestly, and then on the left side of the worksheet under Sandbags, list the sandbags (negative things) that are dragging you down. Some examples are greed, selfishness, or unresolved conflicts (be specific).

2. Put some more honest thought in, and then fill in the Good Things list on the right side of the worksheet. Some examples are good relationships (be specific), joy, or healthy attitudes (in specific areas).

3. Add color to your life balloon—how does the fabric of your life look right now? Is it a muddy gray? Pale yellow? Sickly green? Dark with spots of bright color? Bright with some dark clouds?

4. Sketch a basket that reflects how you feel about the supports in your life. Is the basket big or small? Is it complete or does it lack support in one area or another?

The HOT AIR is the GOOD things in your life that make your life balloon soar.
The four panels of FABRIC holding your balloon together are:
1. Values 2. Character 3. Integrity 4. Morals.
The BASKET that carries you on your journey is made of four sides and a bottom.
1. Family 2. Friends 3. Mentor/Partner 4. Coach & Bottom: Faith and Beliefs.
The SAND BAGS are negative things in your life that pull your life balloon down and keep you from soaring!

Sand Bags:

_____
_____
_____
_____
_____
_____
_____
_____

Good Things:

_____
_____
_____
_____
_____
_____
_____
_____

Worksheet 1

Going Forward

Don't worry if you feel you have a lot of sandbags and not enough good things. In Chapter 7, Goals, you'll see exactly how to cut those sandbags out of your life *and* how to start filling your balloon with the good things that will make it soar.

Okay, you've written down the good and the bad, so let's move on to the next chapter. As you continue through the book and complete each exercise, you can start to erase your sandbags and add more color to your balloon and more items in your good things list.

"Until the pain of staying the same is greater than the pain of change, you will never change." Les Brown

2

Have a Great Attitude!

Want to make an instant change in your life? Have a great attitude!

Easier said than done? Not really. It's all a matter of how you process the things that happen to you. Lou Holtz, the Notre Dame football coach, said, "Life is ten percent what happens to us and ninety percent how we handle it."

When I started in door-to-door sales, I quickly learned what a difference attitude makes not only to how you feel but also to the actual quality of your life. Imagine this scene. I was a young man whose great pleasure in life was good food. I was also starting out at 100 percent commission in door-to-door sales. I had several days of zero sales. What did a zero sales day mean? Zero dollars and obviously not a happy food situation.

So I needed to look at those zero sales days and see what was happening and how to change it. I soon realized that the more negative people I met, the angrier I got. My attitude went into the dumps, and my basket started to sag with sandbags. How many sales do you think an angry man hung all over with negative sandbags can make? If you guessed not many, you guessed right!

So I had to stop letting other people affect my attitude. I needed a great attitude and I needed to hold on to it all day—no matter what happened! I could see about one hundred people a day. If I let the first twenty negative responses drag my attitude down, I was forfeiting my chance with those last eighty potential customers. On the other hand, if I controlled my great attitude all day, I had the same good chance to make a sale to Mr. One Hundred as I had had with Mrs. One.

The technique I discovered that helped me was to end each encounter with a genuine "Have a great day." This closing gave me the power to refuse to internalize the negativity in the situation and to walk away with my great attitude intact.

I had discovered the difference between *reacting* and *responding*. I'll talk more about that in a moment. First, I want you to do the following exercise to help you see the negativity in your life that might be affecting *your* attitude every day. You may be blown away when you see how many negative things you're exposed to on a daily basis. When you start to picture these negatives as sandbags on your life balloon, you'll start to see what's holding you down.

◆ ◆ ◆

CHAPTER 2 EXERCISE 1

For this exercise, you'll use Worksheet 2.

There is a wonderful high-tech concept known as GIGO or Garbage In, Garbage Out. This concept applies to humans as well as computers—the more good you put in the, more good you get out—and unfortunately, it works the same way with the bad stuff.

1. For one day, carry Worksheet 2, The Negativity Log, with you. Write down every single negative expression you *see, hear, say, think,* or *feel*. It's very important that you are able to recognize the negatives. Here are a few examples:

   - "The weather is terrible."
   - "I don't feel well."
   - "That guy is a jerk."

Negativity Log

See	Hear	Say	Think	Feel
Road Rage	This weather is awful	I feel sick to my stomach	My boss is a jerk	I hate that person

Worksheet 2

Now you have a better idea of how much negativity can creep into your life from everyday encounters with your own thoughts, with others, or even with the environment. But what do you do about it?

This is where the difference between *reacting* and *responding* comes in. For example, when a doctor tells you that your body has *reacted* to the medication he gave you, that usually means something bad has happened—a fever, a rash, or some other trouble. Now what if the doctor tells you that your body has *responded* to the medication he gave you? That's a positive thing—you're healing! It is the same in any situation. When you react, it's bad. When you learn to respond, it's good.

Every time you get upset or lose your cool, it is more than likely a reaction. Someone cuts you off in traffic, you get a flat tire, someone is rude to you, and you get angry or frustrated or upset. These are all reactions, and they're not very useful or helpful.

Your brain searches its files to see if you've ever experienced a similar situation and how you handled it. You usually don't take the time to think how to react, you just do.

Responding is the other side of the coin. Responding means that you're evaluating the situation and making a conscious choice to deal with it in the most effective way. You're also going to decide how important situations are so you're not expending too much of your precious life energy on trivial problems.

Here's the technique I developed to respond to life's trials and tribulations. I use a scale from one to ten, one being the least likely to affect the big picture of my life and ten being the most likely to affect the big picture of my life. Where I put challenges on my scale tells me how much negativity or anger it should have in my life at that time.

Here's an example. You go out to start your car and you have a flat tire, so you will certainly be late for work. On my scale, this would be a one, although a reacting person might treat the same situation as a ten.

Here's how I'd process this situation. The tire's flat. What other options do I have? No other car is available so I have to fix the flat. Call the office and let them know I'll be late. Fix the tire and then *forget* about it. I cannot change the fact that the tire is flat. Complaining and kicking the tire and shouting will not repair it. Since time will continue to pass, I might as well change the tire with a smile on my face and be cheerful. At least I woke up today and I can fix a flat tire. That's responding in a nutshell: process the situation, scale it, and move on.

When you use this method over and over, you will soon do it automatically and not even have to think about it.

Let's do another example. Your company downsized, and you just lost your job. Scale it; it would be about a four. Figure out your options: sign up for unemployment to get your checks, and then start looking for another job—maybe even a better one! While you look for another job, take this opportunity to educate yourself. Libraries have books on every subject you might want to explore or stop in at Barnes and Noble, sit in their café, and read all day. Buy, rent, or borrow from the library audiotapes and videotapes on goal setting, communication skills, or strategies for more effective speaking.

You may be wondering that if job loss is only a four, what constitutes a nine or ten? An unexpected fatal tragedy or terminal illness would certainly rank a ten on the scale. Anything less important should not get that much credence. My brother was diagnosed with a brain tumor a few years ago, and when I found out, it was a ten for me. After thinking and praying a lot, I decided that my bad attitude would certainly not help heal the tumor nor would I be of much help to my brother or anyone else. Time would continue to pass whether I was positive or negative. Facing a life-changing event such as this, I certainly did not want time to pass with me continuing to have a bad attitude.

Now you'll get a chance to try rating some of the events in your life.

CHAPTER 2 EXERCISE 2

For this exercise, you'll use Worksheet 3.

You probably have been carrying around some negativity left over from situations in which you reacted rather than responded. For this exercise, you can use an old situation that's still dragging you down or something current. Just be sure the situation is *yours*. It doesn't help you to analyze someone else's life or fictional examples!

1. In the first column, Situation, on Worksheet 3, describe the situation you're going to rate. Use as much detail as you need to get the situation clear in your mind. Remember in one of my examples, I didn't just have a flat tire; I was also going to be late for work. The same situation on a weekday or a weekend can feel very different.

2. In the second column, rate the situation. Remember you're *responding*, not reacting. Give the situation the real rating it deserves in your life.

3. In the third column, write down the response the situation requires. This column will include all of the things you need to do to *finish* the situation and move on.

4. Use the second row to work through another situation. If you used a family example in the first row, you might want to choose a work situation for the second one.

Rate a Situation

Situation	Rate It (1–10)	What's Your Response?
1. *Flat tire*	*2*	*Call work and let them know I'll be late, fix the tire, and notice the sunshine*
2		

Worksheet 3

If you live another day, you will surely be able to handle whatever comes next, especially now that you'll be responding instead of reacting. Attitude goes a long way to help you remember to respond. Zig Ziglar, one of the greatest motivational speakers is quoted "Attitude will determine your altitiude". Attitude is everything!

To help you find a better attitude, the next exercise focuses on the good things in your life. You'll fill in Worksheet 4, Things I'm Grateful For. I think you'll be surprised by all the good things in your life that you overlook or take for granted.

◆   ◆   ◆

CHAPTER 2 EXERCISE 3

For this exercise, you'll use Worksheet 4.

This exercise is so simple that it doesn't really need an introduction. You're going to examine your life and pick out *all* of the things for which you're grateful. Don't worry, you'll find lots once you get going!

5. On a blank piece of paper (don't use Worksheet 4 yet), write down everything that's good in your life. Don't stop until you've filled at least one page. After that, continue through as many pages as you need until you're finished. Some examples are my family, my best friend, food on the table, the gift of hearing so I can listen to rain or the laughter of children, the gift of sight so I can see my child or a sunset, the gift of smell so I can enjoy the aroma of spring or the warm scent of a puppy, freedom, snow, birds. Your list won't look like anyone else's.

6. Now select the things that are most meaningful to you and copy them onto Worksheet 4. Post the page somewhere in your house so you can look at it before you start your day.

Gratitude List

1. _____
2. _____
3. _____
4. _____
5. _____
6. _____
7. _____
8. _____
9. _____
10. _____
11. _____
12. _____
13. _____
14. _____
15. _____
16. _____
17. _____
18. _____
19. _____
20. _____
21. _____
22. _____
23. _____
24. _____
25. _____
26. _____
27. _____
28. _____
29. _____
30. _____
31. _____
32. _____
33. _____
34. _____
35. _____
36. _____
37. _____
38. _____
39. _____
40. _____
41. _____
42. _____

Worksheet 4

Going Forward

Reading your gratitude list day after day will soon start a change in your attitude. The petty things that used to upset you and affect your attitude will no longer be thorns in your side. Sandbags will start to drop off your balloon simply because appreciation chokes out negativity, which is obviously a big, heavy sandbag. You will have to work at it, but the rewards are endless when you learn to control your attitude.

If your grateful list is not long enough, I suggest you volunteer at a children's burn unit, feed the homeless at a soup kitchen, volunteer at a nursing home, or watch an hour of television to see how people in developing countries live. I know some of this might be drastic, but look at the flip side of not developing a great attitude, the tragedy of wasting time by having a bad attitude.

I would like to clarify something before I close this chapter. A bad attitude is not grumbling and shouting all the time; a bad attitude is when you lose hope and you start to believe that nothing will ever go your way. Decide to change your attitude today. Remember, time passes whether you're smiling or frowning. Don't waste even a second on the latter.

Your life balloon's altitude is determined by your attitude.

3

GoodFinding

You've heard about finding the silver lining in the clouds; being a goodfinder is doing just that. The first time I came across the word *goodfinder* was in Dale Carnegie's book *How to Win Friends and Influence People*. In this chapter you will work on developing your "goodfinding" skills and making them part of your everyday life.

Here is a simple story that will show you what this concept looks like in practice. One day, a master and his disciples were walking on a hot, dusty dirt road and discussing life. Soon they saw something in the road. As they got closer, they realized it was a dog that had met his fate. Due to the sun and the natural process of decay, the dog was not a pretty sight, and the disciples were disturbed by what they had found. The master looked down at the dog and said, "Look at those incredibly white, perfect teeth."

Now that's what I call goodfinding.

Goodfinding works for troublesome situations and troublesome relationships. Because it's easier to practice this skill with situations, you'll start there. Here's an example. A man was fired from his ninth job in five years. What could possibly be the good in that situation? Well, the next job he got, instead of being just another in a string of unrewarding positions, was working for someone who became his mentor. The man and his new mentor eventually became partners and built a multibillion-dollar company. So the goodfinding in the firing was that he was free to pursue the next opportunity when it came along.

Obviously, the "good" in every situation will not be that obvious. The point is that everything has something good in it. You can find it if you are looking for the good and not dwelling on the bad. As with all the skills you're learning, the more you practice goodfinding, the more automatic it becomes.

Goodfinding helps control the environment you carry with you. Picture your life balloon. No matter where it travels, through storms, rain, or wind, the environment inside your basket is positive and powered by goodfinding.

Here is another example of goodfinding in a work situation. My nephew is handicapped; he doesn't walk or talk. But he loves to go to Disney World because there, he is king. He is the first in line for all the rides. He gets the red carpet treatment from the Disney staff. Everything is focused to help him have fun. The staff at Disney could easily have seen physically challenged children as more work, but instead they looked for the good. They saw the idea of accessibility as an opportunity for Disney to bring light to children with problems. Disney isn't just accessible; it's a wonderland for kids like my nephew.

If you or people in your business have struggled with handicapped accessibility issues, look to the Disney model to see how you can turn this situation (or others) around using goodfinding.

Now it's time for a test run.

◆ ◆ ◆

CHAPTER 3 EXERCISE 1

For this exercise, you'll use Worksheet 5.

In this exercise, you'll be a goodfinder in a situation from your life. Don't use a person or a human relationship—that's coming in the next exercise. In this one focus on a situation that's external and inanimate like your morning commute or paying your bills.

1. Worksheet 5 is divided into two sections. In the top section, write down a situation that occurred recently that you think could have benefited from goodfinding. Be sure to use lots of details to help you really get into the same frame of mind. For example, someone might write down her morning commute. The traffic is usually backed up, stop and start for seven miles. The other drivers are aggressive, and the drive is very stressful.

2. In the second column, explore your attitudes and feelings about that situation before you tried goodfinding. In the commute example, the person might write down anger at other drivers, frustration with a boss who refuses to consider flextime, anxiety about safety.

3. In the last column, detail the concrete negatives in terms of wasted time or other unhealthy consequences that arise from the way you've been thinking about this situation. In the commute example, this might be a stressful start to each workday with stiff muscles or angry feelings that linger throughout the day.

4. Now in the bottom half of the worksheet do a goodfinding on the situation. In the first column, write down any good you can find in the situation. If you have to, start small. But be sure you find something good. The frustrated commuter might write down that the commute offers an hour of quiet time without having to talk to other people or that the commute carries her past a gorgeous tree each October.

5. In the middle column, list your feelings about the situation after the goodfinding.

6. In the last column, write down what you can envision as the positive effects of your new feelings or outlook.

Goodfinding in a Situation

Situation	My Attitude and Feelings (Before Goodfinding)	Time Wasted or Other Unhealthy Consequences
Lost my job	*Anger, fear*	*24 hours a day every day, stress, fatigue, feeling of hopelessness*

Goodfinding	My Attitude and Feelings (After Goodfinding)	Time Saved or Other Healthy Consequences
Lost my job	*Fired up, excited about a new beginning and finding something better*	*24 hours a day every day, optimism, hopeful*

Worksheet 5

Now for the harder skill, goodfinding with people you know! People—you're surrounded by them. People are in every part of your life, from the time you wake up until the time you go to bed. People are everywhere, and you must interact with them.

Goodfinding in people is just what it sounds like—looking for the good in people. Whether you like them does not matter. The older I get, the more I realize how fast time goes by. And yet, it's easy to get caught up in life instead of living it to the fullest.

I like to be in a positive environment, even if the environment is the few minutes it takes to buy a cup of coffee. By goodfinding, you can transport your positive environment with you wherever you go. If you begin the habit of goodfinding in situations and in people, you will see things start to change. You will actually get to another level of transforming your sandbags into good things as opposed to cutting the bags loose.

As an employer, I dreaded seeing a particular person every morning. He was dramatic about the smallest thing and complained about everything. Initially my focus was on his faults. Every day I reinforced this in my own head with thoughts such as, "Boy, that person is annoying and so negative, I can barely stand to be around him for more than thirty seconds." All I expected from my encounters with this person was annoyance.

But I was not willing to give up on my positive environment, so even though it was difficult, I started goodfinding. I was looking for something in that person that I could compliment on or that I could focus on in a positive way.

Before long, I found that good thing I could focus on, for this person it was his work ethic and loyalty. From that point on, my dealings with him, from my point of view, were much more positive. At least, I didn't dread talking with him. That doesn't mean that the person automatically stopped the complaining and drama; what it meant was that, because I focused on his good points, it made the conversation much more positive. I know he felt the shift in my mood to the positive when I started goodfinding. I never told him what I was doing; I just did it. I always tried to look at him positively instead of negatively. Not only did I drop some of my sandbags, but his sandbags also started to fall off simply because of the way I treated him. It's all about soaring, for you and for the people around you.

I try to use goodfinding with every situation and person in my life. Certainly some situations are harder than others, but the end result will be worth the effort you have to put in. Your life will be much more positive and your attitude will be more in your control.

Here is another example of the power of goodfinding; I heard it at a meeting some time ago. A teacher in a high school had each student stand in front of the class one by one. As each student stood up, the rest of the class was instructed to say, *I like Tommy because...* The compliments varied from his sweater, to his smile, to his handwriting. It didn't matter what the other students said as long as it was a compliment.

As the students said these things out loud, the teacher wrote them down on a piece of paper. At the end of class the teacher handed each student the piece of paper that said *I like so and so because...* Fast-forward a few years. The Vietnam War breaks out, and among the casualties was one of the students who'd participated in the exercise. The teacher attended the funeral, and at the end of the service, the grieving mother recognized the teacher and started to thank her for the influence the teacher had in her son's life. The mother told the teacher that when his belongings were sent back from Vietnam, in his wallet was the crumpled piece of paper listing those long-ago compliments. Other students from that same class were listening to the conversation. One by one, they pulled out their pieces of paper. Then they told their stories of the little paper had given them the hope to pick themselves back up again at the lowest points of their lives.. That is the power of goodfinding.

Now take a shot at goodfinding with some of the troublesome people in your life.

♦ ♦ ♦

Chapter 3 Exercise 2

For this exercise, you'll use Worksheet 6.

In this exercise, you'll see how to carry your own good environment with you, how to be a people builder, and how to make other people feel great about themselves.

1. At the top of Worksheet 6, write the name of your goodfinding target. Choose someone you run into every day or every week. Be sure it's someone you're not particularly excited to see. (Goodfinding with a good friend is too easy!)

2. Next, write down five things you like or admire about the person. Some examples may be the way they dress, how they treat their kids, or the poise they show in staff meetings. This exercise is not supposed to be easy! If you have trouble filling in the five blanks, that's good—just work harder. Something will come to you.

3. When your list is complete, memorize it. The next time you see this person, remember the five things and focus on them when you're interacting.

Goodfinding in a Person

Name of Goodfinding Target: _____

Five Good Things

1. _____

2. _____

3. _____

4. _____

5. _____

Worksheet 6

Going Forward

Goodfinding is one of the harder skills to master when it involves a person you knew before you started changing your attitude. You may be so used to looking only at the person's negatives that every time she does something to reinforce that negativity it'll hard not to focus on it. But with discipline you can master this skill. Keep goodfinding.

Here is a fun way to practice. The next time you go out to eat, find out your server's name. When you leave the money for the bill, include a note saying, "I like [server's name] because _____." Don't just make something up; look for the good during your meal and find something true. When you walk out, try to find a spot where the server can't see you. You'll be amazed and elated to see his or her reaction to your note.

When it's working, you won't just drop off the negative sandbag; you will transform it into the good stuff because you are helping another person. It's like a videogame; if you get extra keys, your character gets more power.

The more people you help, the higher your balloon gets to soar.

4

Relationships

Relationships—you all have them, bad and good. But have you thought about how relationships affect not only your life but the person you become?

Here is a story to illustrate the power a relationship can have. There was a boy who had a disease that made his back bowed instead of straight. His father was the king of the land, but the boy stayed out of sight because of his back. The father erected a statue of his son showing the boy standing up straight. The statue didn't show how the boy actually looked; it showed how his father saw him. Every day the boy would go out to the courtyard and look at the statue. He would try to stand straight just like the statue, sometimes stretching until it hurt. Day after day, month after month, this boy would look at the statue and try to stand straight despite the agonizing pain. On the boy's twenty-first birthday, the king threw him a party and the whole kingdom came. When the guest of honor appeared from behind a curtain, he was standing as straight as the statue.

Now, picture the same story except the king was a negative, ungrateful person. Every time he saw his son, day after day, month after month, the king berated him, and called him names. The father never erected a statue of his son, and as in the previous story, the son hid from the rest of the kingdom. In this story, however, there is no happy ending. The son stayed hidden for the rest of his days.

What's the lesson in these two stories? The way family and friends see you can be the downfall or the victory in your life.

In the first version of the story, the father pictured his son as how he could be, which influenced the son to become that person. In the second version, the father saw his son as a hunchback and that is the way he stayed. In the good story, the father filled his son's balloon with great stuff; in the negative story, the father loaded his son's basket to overflowing.

Both versions of this story are acted out every day in some part of the world. I can't stress enough the importance of the people who influence your life. The way friends and family see you can be good or bad. Sometimes the people who care for you the most are the ones who can be most negative. Sometimes their negativity even starts from good intentions.

Sometimes your family or your spouse may be trying to protect you from disappointment or failure or frustration when he or she tells you that you can't do something, that it's too hard or dangerous, that it won't work. Maybe they are just afraid, and so they give things a negative spin.

Because you don't want to shut your family out of your life, sometimes the best thing to do is to make a conscious decision about how much information you give them. This isn't lying. It's learning to keep your mouth shut about possibilities and only opening it when there is a reality to share.

For example, say you're developing a new product in your garage. You've studied products that would be your competition and you think your idea is great. But if you tell your family at the idea stage, they may tell you "that will never work," "you're wasting your time," "do you know how big those other companies are?" So don't tell them right away. Wait until you make your first sale and then share your achievement. This is a way of protecting your brain from too much negativity. When you constantly hear negatives, your brain tends to repeat them anytime you attempt to do something new.

Walt Disney's first boss told him he had no talent, vision, or future as a cartoonist. What if Walt had listened to that man instead of listening to himself? Walt Disney's life balloon was magnificent. He took his dream and created a life-giving place for children and families. He wasn't just filling his own balloon; he was making a place where other people could fill theirs.

Of course, you may have people outside your family who affect your life in a negative way. They may be friends, coworkers, or just daily contacts like the mail carrier or door attendant at work. If the people in your life are not striving to make their lives better while you are growing and working on your life, you may find that they turn into sandbags and keep your balloon grounded for life.

If you are satisfied with your place in life, there is nothing wrong with those kinds of relationships. On the other hand, if you want to soar, you <u>must</u> hang around like-minded, positive people. If some of your relationships involve people who are negative because of low self-esteem, help them see the positive side of things. But keep in mind what the airline attendants say in the beginning of the flight, "If we should encounter a problem with the aircraft, oxygen masks will drop down in front of you. If you are traveling with a child, make sure you put your mask on first and then the child's." In other words, you have to be in the right position to be able to help someone else in need. If you're struggling with life, don't call a friend who is headed in the same direction, work on yourself and then go back to help.

Misery loves company. Eleanor Roosevelt said, "No one can make you feel inferior without your consent." My version of this quote is "Nobody can load sandbags into your basket without your permission." You need to be careful of the company you keep, especially if the other person is jealous and is afraid you might do better. Those relationships only get worse.

There are many people out there who value every day and are thankful for everything. When you find these people, hang on to them, find their interests, and start developing a relationship. Being around positive people who have the same foresight as you will impact your life and provide support that you can only imagine. Make a list of the people you have met in the past twelve months who stick out in your mind as being positive. Get in contact with them by e-mail or phone, and ask them if they would like to grab a cup of coffee. Be up-front about why you called them. Let them know you felt they were very positive and seemed to have a great outlook on life and that you'd like to bounce ideas off them every once in a while. They will appreciate the compliment and the honesty, and it will be the beginning of a new, positive relationship. I have done this on a number of occasions and it works great.

Find people who have the same morals and values as you, people who are working on bettering their place in life, and attach yourself to them. You will see your whole attitude and way of life change the minute you move on. Imagine surrounding yourself with people builders instead of people wreckers. Imagine the long-term effects being positive and having positive relationships will have on your children. Not only will you set an example, but you also will create an environment that will be filled with good things and positive growth for the people around you.

◆ ◆ ◆

CHAPTER 4 EXERCISE 1

For this exercise, you'll use Worksheet 7.

In this exercise, you're going to do an honest evaluation of the relationships you have with the people in your life. You might be surprised by the results! The purpose of this exercise is to help you get the most out of your life, so you'll need to be honest.

1. Fill in the Name and Relationship columns in the table for a person with whom you have a relationship—for example, your spouse or your secretary.

2. In the Frequency of Contact column, write down how often you encounter the person—for example, daily, weekly, monthly, or only on family holidays!

3. Now it's time to do your hard thinking. Put a + or – in the last column, indicating whether the relationship is positive or negative for you. Does this person build you up or tear you down? Help you soar higher or weight you down with sandbags?

4. Repeat the first three steps for each person you're in contact with. Don't forget anyone—even the guy at the coffee shop who's negative every morning may be affecting your life.

5. Once you complete your list, it's decision time. How much of a role and how much importance should you allow the people who are consistently negative? If one relationship seems clearly troubling, it may be time to cut the rope holding your balloons together. There's no need to tell this person that you're ending your relationship because of his or her negativity, but some people do benefit from that information if it's communicated sensitively. The decision is yours.

People in Your Life

Name	Relationship	+ or -	Frequency of Contact
Joe	*Coworker*	*-*	*Daily*

Worksheet 7

Going Forward

Recognizing when a relationship is dragging you down is one of those skills that take practice. You're going to need to work to build this skill into the fabric of your life. Don't let it drift away. Once again, the decision is yours. Remember that the decision you make today could affect the altitude of your life balloon a year or more from now.

If you want to fly with the eagles, you can't hang out with the turkeys.

5

Self-Talk

I want you to picture yourself standing in your basket, reaching over the side and loading sandbag after sandbag into your basket until there is no more room to stand. That's what negative self-talk can do to you and your life balloon.

Self-talk is not something you hear about at the water cooler at work, but it's extremely powerful in deciding how soon (if ever) you will reach your goals. The problem with self-talk is most of it is very negative and it's automatic. Think about any time you decided to try something new or were involved in a competition. What was your subconscious telling you over and over? You can't do this…don't screw it up…you don't deserve this…you're not smart enough…you don't have enough money…you're too old. You didn't even have to leave your house to get a good mental whooping.

Think about two athletes in a competition. They have the same talents, size, practice schedules. The competition comes down to the final minutes. What decides who will win? Often, self-talk is the decision maker.

The winner is not always the better athlete but the one who learns that what is going on in his or her head and deals with it. That is why only a handful of people ever reach great heights. They have learned how not only to control what their brain is saying, but they're able to reprogram and automatically talk themselves into the winner's circle.

"I think I can, I think I can, I know I can, I know I can." Those sentences made famous by a children's book about the little engine that could are the kind of talk you need to get into the habit of doing all the time.

I'm not talking about inflating your ego. I'm talking about knowing your abilities and talents and then using them without hesitation and with the belief that they are sufficient to accomplish whatever it is you need to do. Bad habits are not easy to break. It's hard work, but it's well worth the outcome of losing those heavy sandbags.

The way our brain works is similar to a computer search engine. When you think of a word or situation, your brain will check all the folders to find something similar. If it can't find the exact phrase, it will get something close but always with the same result: negative. If you're not aware of what's going on behind the scenes, you'll take your brain's word for it and act or not act depending on the automatic response you get.

I'm sure that you now realize the awesome power self-talk has and how it can make or break your life. Okay, now let's see how to fix it. Step 1 is to catch yourself talking negatively to yourself. It's pretty easy if you take time to listen instead of being on automatic. Step 2 is to stop what you're doing, grab the Self-Talk Log (Worksheet 8) and follow the directions. I know that every opportunity may not be the best time to do this, especially if it's your first performance doing a high wire act at the circus. But the more you practice, the better you'll get at defeating negative self-talk.

Until you get to be an expert positive self-talker, you can turn to outside help. Find a positive thinking tape that works for you. Listen to the tape to and from work every day. This will continually fills your balloon with the good stuff, and you can never have enough good air in your balloon. I cannot stress enough the importance of positive self-talk. When computers first came out, I always heard GIGO, which stands for garbage in, garbage out. The opposite is true. If you can train yourself to do positive self-talk, you'll have good in, good out instead.

CHAPTER 5 EXERCISE 1

For this exercise, you'll use Worksheet 8.

Use the Self-Talk Log for at least one week. Focus particularly on times when you're involved in a presentation, going out on a first date, starting a new job, or asking someone for something you want.

1. In the first column, name the event that triggered the self-talk. You don't have to use a formal name. It could be something like "Conversation with Betsy."

2. In the second column, write down your self-talk. Be as honest and comprehensive as you can. You might feel ashamed to write down some of the things you "told" yourself, but the road to growth leads through honest evaluation. Some examples of self-talk around a work presentation might be "I can't do this," "I don't like my voice," "the presentation isn't good enough."

3. In the third column, put a + or – to show if the self-talk was positive or negative.

4. In the fourth column, decide if the self-talk statements are true or false. For example, before doing a work presentation, you told yourself the presentation was too short. Go back through your notes and evaluate it. Did you cover the topics thoroughly? Did you present all the pertinent facts? Did you practice it to be sure it would fit within the allotted time? After thinking it through, you can decide if your self-talk was true or false.

5. If the self-talk was true, you might need to make an action plan to provide practice for a particular area of your life. (This is covered in Chapter 7, Goals.) But if the self-talk was *false* (most of it is),

then in the final column, make a list of the credentials/skills/qualities you possess that make you equal to the challenge. List all the reasons you are qualified, even if they are minor.

Self-Talk Log

Event	Self-Talk	+ or -	True or False	Credentials
Speech at Wedding	*I don't know what to say. I'm going to make a fool of myself*	*-*	*False*	*I've known the person my whole life and will talk about that.*

Worksheet 8

Going Forward

If you use your self-talk log every time you face a situation that starts your negative self-talk yapping, you will be able to break the pattern of negative self-talk. Keep your list of talents and abilities close at hand so you can work on positive self-talk. (It's strange to say that you may need reminders about *your* best qualities! But it's often true.)

Once you have a handle on positive self-talk, you can start to pump up the good air in your balloon by sharing this skill with others in your life. When you see someone struggling with negative self-talk (they'll be the ones hesitating or looking uneasy before a new experience), encourage them with some thoughts about their abilities or gifts. Show them where to find their positive self-talk. You'll help them throw out some sandbags and fill your own balloon even more with good air to soar. Something I read that sticks out in my mind: *"Watch your thoughts; they become your words. Watch your words; they become actions. Watch your actions; they become habits. Watch your habits; they become character. Watch your character; it becomes your destiny." Frank Outlaw*

6

Problem Solving

I know the title of this chapter is not politically correct. The best-known speakers in the motivation world like to put a positive spin on problems and call them *challenges*. In one sense, I agree because words can be very powerful and have a tremendous effect on how you handle situations. But, for the sake of this chapter, let's call a duck a duck and a problem a problem. You will learn how to cut those *problem* sandbags from your basket and soar.

You encounter problems every single day from minor ones (e.g., not the car's out of gas and you're running late for work) to more serious ones (e.g., your car's been stolen or you lost job and you don't have enough money to get by). My hope is that you make it a part of your life and pass it along to others. Once this skill becomes automatic, you will see your stress sandbags drop off the side of your basket.

This chapter centers around recognizing what problems are *real* right now in your life and what problems you can *solve*. If a problem isn't real or it's not something you can solve, there is no sense worrying about it. You'll whittle your list of problems down to include only real, solvable ones, and then you'll be ready to tackle some of them and find solutions.

So you're going to learn to separate your problems into two categories: real and possible. Most of what you worry about will never happen. So you can see that identifying the problems that are real is an important step. If you can identify exactly what the problems are, you won't waste time on anything that is not real. For example, if my problem is that I might lose my job or my car might break down and I won't have the money to get it fixed, I need to see if those problems are real. If my boss has not said anything to me about my job and my car has been running great, these so-called problems are just possibilities. They're not real and I shouldn't be wasting time with them.

So the first skill is to identify the real problems and the next is to identify the problems that you can solve. An example of a no-solution problem is your wife is stuck at an airport that is shut down because of weather. You can't solve that problem—you have no control over the weather or the air traffic controllers.

Here's an example of a problem that has a solution. Your car is sitting in the driveway and won't start. The solution is to call a tow truck or have a mechanically inclined friend come over and fix it.

These are simple illustrations to help you understand how to cut through the worry and look at the actual situation. Once you've identified your real problems and the solutions, you need to practice prioritizing. Take care of the most urgent problems first. I've used this step-by-step approach over the course of my lifetime, especially in sales. Here's another story to show you the value of prioritizing. I was working with another person one day and the area we were working had just been worked by someone else from the office. This is very discouraging. Most people would have gone back to the office and complained about the duplication of effort. But I got a local map and picked another area. The problem was that I didn't have a sales territory and I needed to let the office know about the mix-up. But for a commission salesperson, finding the territory was the most pressing problem; the office work could wait.

If my car had broken down on the way to my territory, I would have had two problems: a broken car and no way to get to my territory. Again, my priority was to sell, so instead of spending time trying to fix my car, I would have found a way to sell that day and then worried about fixing the car. If I'd finished selling and had made some money, the car would still have been there and I would still have been able to get a tow truck. But if I had spent my day taking care of the car, I wouldn't have been able to get my sales in.

So there is the problem pulverizer, simple but extremely powerful. There is something that happens to you when you get things on paper. It's equivalent to dropping sandbags off your basket, especially when you're writing down problems—just that exercise alone will take tremendous weight off your life balloon. When you are able to identify your problems, you'll soon realize that most of them are more of a nuisance than a life-altering dilemma, but that only will happen when you take the time to grab the pen and paper and write them down. Then and only then will the stress start to lessen, the sandbags will drop off, and your balloon will begin to rise.

◆ ◆ ◆

CHAPTER 6 EXERCISE 1

For this exercise, you'll use Worksheet 9.
Here is a great exercise for dropping sandbags quickly!

1. In the first column, jot down a description of the problem.

2. In the second column, identify the problem as real or possible. (Real problems are actually happening or will definitely happen. All the others are possibilities.)

3. At this point, cross out any problem that is not real. You don't need to deal with it anymore.

4. If the problem is real, mark it as either a solution or as no solution in the third column. For problems with a solution, include the steps you'll need to take.

5. Cross off any problems that don't have a solution. You can't do anything about them.

6. In the last column, create a problem-solving timetable. Prioritize your problems and write down a date (or time) when you will solve each one. Remember to think about what *you* need when you set the problem priorities.

Problem Pulverizer Worksheet (Stress Releaser)

Problem	Real or Possible?	Solution or No Solution?	Action Timetable
$200 short on bills/month	Real	Solution: Par- time job, work out budget, and cut out luxuries	Today's Date

Worksheet 9

Going Forward

There is something that happens when you get things down on paper. It's the equivalent of dropping sandbags from your basket, especially when you're writing down problems. Just using the pulverizer once will take a tremendous weight off your life balloon. When you are able to identify your problems specifically, you'll soon realize that most of them are more of a nuisance than a life-altering dilemma, but that only will happen when you take the time to grab the pen and paper and write them down. Then and only then will the stress start to lessen, the sandbags will drop off, and your balloon will begin to ascend.

The problem pulverizer is simple but extremely powerful.

7

Goals

According to a Harvard survey of their 1979 MBA graduates, only 3 percent of Americans set goals. And yet, goal setting is another simple skill that is so powerful when it is done consistently and correctly. In this chapter, you'll find lots of examples and pointers for setting goals and then several worksheets you can use to set your own goals and start achieving changes!

For a balanced life balloon, you should concentrate on setting goals in these areas:

1. Family/friends
2. Career
3. Financial
4. Spiritual
5. Physical
6. Lifelong learning or self-education

At the end of the chapter, you will write your goals from these six areas on your Life Balloon Map and then on your goal cards.

One of the first steps toward effective goal setting is learning to recognize the difference between a dream and a goal. A goal is a specific objective, whereas a dream is a general wish. That's why the first step—identifying specific targeted outcomes—is the most important. Here's an example.

Let's say you're a newlywed and you and your spouse decide you want to buy a house. Okay, if you stopped there, that is only a dream. Here's how to make it a goal. Be specific and write down the type of house (bedrooms, bathrooms, basement), land, neighborhood, price range, school district, and any other criteria that are important to you.

Once you come up with all the details, you should have it narrowed down to the price range that you would be able to afford comfortably. Figure out the down payment you need. For this exercise, let's say the house you would like is $150,000. For a 5 percent down payment, you would need $7,500, plus say another $2,500 in closing costs. Your total goal is $10,000.

Next figure out all your bills and how much you have left over to put toward your new house. Maybe this number is $500/month if you sacrifice some luxuries, like going out to eat or buying expensive clothes, for a while. Break it down even more: When you get paid weekly, you will have to set aside $125. Then open up a "new house" bank account and every payday deposit $125 into this account. After twenty months, you will have saved enough money for your down payment on your first house. Next you may want to set a five-year goal to trade up to a better house. Repeat the same process and figure out how much you need to save. This process is the one you will use for every part of your life.

There are so many formulas and ways that people explain how to use goals that my goal is to keep it very simple and straightforward. I use the acronym ASCEND to keep the steps in my mind.

1. **Ascertain and specify** what you want your life to be like in each of the six areas I mentioned. This will be your life map when it's completed.

2. **Set** the goals in terms of importance; you want to choose the ones that will have the greatest impact on your life and your family.

3. **Classify** them into three categories: short, medium, and long term. The short-term goals can be weekly or monthly. (One of the nice thing about goals is you can use them in a way that will be most

effective for *your* life.) I always make medium-term goals one to three years. Long-term goals are five years.

4. **Establish** your action plan. Work backward from your goal and develop your action plan. Once you know the steps to be taken, you'll break them down even more in step 5.

5. **Nail** the steps down into daily tasks. These will be things you do on a daily basis that will get you one day closer to your goal.

6. **Do it!**

Let's get started!

◆ ◆ ◆

CHAPTER 7 EXERCISE 1

For this exercise, you'll use Worksheet 10.

In this exercise, you're going to find out exactly what you want from your life. This is a step midway between dreaming and targeted goal setting. Use your creative side to think about these questions and see what comes out when you're honest about what you want. You are not setting specific goals in this exercise. That comes later.

1. Complete the questions on Worksheet 10, Design Your Life Balloon. There are a lot of questions so take your time—break your session up if you have to.

Design Your Life Balloon

If you could be anyone you wanted to be, who would it be and why?

_____

_____

If you could live anywhere in the world, where would it be and why?

_____

_____

If you could do whatever you wanted in life, what would it be?

_____

_____

If you could afford the house of your dreams, what would it look like?

_____

_____

If you could afford the car of your dreams, what would it be?

_____

_____

If you could choose the perfect mate, what would that person be like?

_____

_____

If you could choose the perfect family, what would they be like?

_____

_____

If you could have the best possible family life, what would that be like?

_____

_____

If you could have the best possible social life, what would that be like?

_____

_____

If you could know one thing that you don't know now, what would that be?

_____

_____

If you could be in terrific physical shape, what would that be?

If you could be more spiritual, how would you act differently?

If you could select your friends, what would they be like?

If you could earn as much money as you desired, how much would that be?

If you could have any position in business, what would it be?

Say you won the lottery and had all the money you would ever need, what would you do?

_____

_____

If you found Aladdin's lamp and the genie granted you three wishes, what would they be?

_____

_____

What does success mean to you?

_____

_____

Now, go back to each of your answers and ask the following questions:

1. Is it possible to live the way I would like to?
2. How can I make these dreams come true?
3. Can I achieve these dreams doing what I'm doing now?

Now you've got a big picture of what you'd like your life to be like. You need to create targeted goals to help you get to your new place. For this you'll use Worksheet 11, Setting Your Goals.

♦   ♦   ♦

CHAPTER 7 EXERCISE 2

For this exercise, you'll use Worksheet 11.

This worksheet helps you classify your goals into short term, medium term, and long term. This is the first step toward putting together a game plan.

1. Review your answers to the questions in Worksheet 10. Decide which of those answers you'd like to turn into goals (targets).

2. On Worksheet 11, Setting Your Goals, list five short-term targets. Be sure to prioritize them. (Short-term targets can be reached in less than a month.)

3. List five medium-term targets and then prioritize them. (Medium-term targets can be reached in one to three years.)

4. List long-term targets and then prioritize them. (Long-term targets can be reached in less than five years.)

5. Break out your goals into the six areas—Spiritual, Career, Financial, Family/Friends, Physical, and Personal Growth—and write them on your life balloon map and then on your goal cards, which you can carry or place on your sun visor.

Setting Your Goals Worksheet

It's extremely important to form the habit of targeting, so begin with short-range targets that can provide small successes. As you continue to accomplish your short-range targets, you can move on to medium-range and long-range targets. Your goals should all build on one another.

Short-range targets:
1._____
2._____
3._____
4._____
5._____

Targets in priority order:
1._____
2._____
3._____
4._____
5._____

Medium-range targets:
1._____
2._____
3._____
4._____
5._____

Targets in priority order:
1._____
2._____
3._____
4._____
5._____

Long-range targets:
1._____
2._____
3._____
4._____
5._____

Targets in priority order:
1._____
2._____
3._____
4._____
5._____

Worksheet 11

Life Balloon Map

Family/Friends
_____
_____
_____

Career
_____
_____
_____

Financial
_____
_____
_____

Spiritual
_____
_____
_____

Physical
_____
_____
_____

Lifelong Learning
_____
_____
_____

Goal Cards

Make Your Life Balloon Soar!
Financial Goal Card
By: _____
    Month   Day   Year
_____
_____
_____
www.wehelpyouachieve.com
800-771-2275 copyright©dwrobel 2004

Make Your Life Balloon Soar!
Spiritual Goal Card
By: _____
    Month   Day   Year
_____
_____
_____
www.wehelpyouachieve.com
800-771-2275 copyright©dwrobel 2004

Make Your Life Balloon Soar!
Physical Goal Card
By: _____
    Month   Day   Year
_____
_____
_____
www.wehelpyouachieve.com
800-771-2275 copyright©dwrobel 2004

Make Your Life Balloon Soar!
Lifelong Learning Goal Card
By: _____
    Month   Day   Year
_____
_____
_____
www.wehelpyouachieve.com
800-771-2275 copyright©dwrobel 2004

Make Your Life Balloon Soar!
Family/Friend Goal Card
By: _____
    Month   Day   Year
_____
_____
_____
www.wehelpyouachieve.com
800-771-2275 copyright© dwrobel 2004

Make Your Life Balloon Soar!
Career Goal Card
By: _____
    Month   Day   Year
_____
_____
_____
www.wehelpyouachieve.com
800-771-2275 copyright©dwrobel 2004

Now you're really getting your goal targeted down to actual steps. The last step is to fill out Worksheet 12, Goals Worksheet. Here is an example to show you how to use the Goals Worksheet. My seven-year-old daughter set a goal to improve her handwriting within the next year. Using the worksheet, her statement of goal would be "I will improve my handwriting to be legible and neat." She will benefit from better grades, improve her self-confidence, experience bettering herself through practice, find inner discipline, and feel a sense of accomplishment by achieving her goal. Her specific action step was to practice writing every night by completing a handwriting worksheet. When she completed the night of work, she checked the box that corresponded to the task. As the days passed and she continued to practice, her writing dramatically improved. This is a simple illustration, but it shows the functional ability of goal setting.

Now, my daughter could have set up her action steps in terms of a time limit—say, thirty minutes of practicing letters or she could have done two worksheets a night. She might have set her action steps as a choice—either thirty minutes of practice or a worksheet. Whatever way you have to package it to keep yourself motivated is the way you set it up.

Let's do another one. Maybe you've realized you don't spend a lot of quality time with your child. So let's define it. I want my relationship with my child (use his or her name) to be one of mutual trust, fun, and learning about each other. Okay. Now how do you get there? You work a lot and have other commitments but there is a forty-five-minute period every day before your child's bedtime that is free.

Okay, that's the time slot; now make an action step. On Monday night, play cards for a half hour and spend the last fifteen minutes reading a story. Tuesday night is video game night. Wednesday is TV night. Thursday is "learn something new" night, and so on until you've done all the days of the week.

CHAPTER 7 EXERCISE 3

For this exercise, you'll use Worksheet 12.

This worksheet is the nitty-gritty of goal setting. Be sure you are clear and honest about what you can accomplish.

1. Select one of the medium-term goals you identified and fill in the Statement of Goal section on the Goals Worksheet.

2. Fill in today's date and your final target date.

3. Clearly state all the ways you will benefit from achieving this goal. Be specific and think hard. It might get tough to stick to your goal and the benefits will help keep you motivated.

4. Fill in the action steps section at the bottom of the worksheet. Break your tasks down into manageable segments.

5. Keep this sheet where you can see it, refer to it often, and check those action steps off as you get to them!

Goals Worksheet

| Today's Date: | Final Target Date: | Date Achieved: |

Statement of Goal:
I will weigh 200 pounds

In What Ways Will I Benefit from Achieving this Goal?
I will live longer, I will have more energy, I will be able to play more with my children, I will have a better self-image, I will be more self-confident, my clothes will fit better

Specific Action Steps for Achieving This Goal:	Target Date:	Complete
1. *Decide on Diet or Method of Weight Loss*		
2.		☐
3.		☐
4.		☐
5.		☐
		☐

Worksheet 12

Going Forward

Use goal setting to improve your knowledge, relationships, or income, or to lose weight, buy a car, or go on vacation. The key to make this all work is to anchor the goals to something that will tug at your heartstrings when you lose motivation to continue. Using the previous example, you get home from work one night and you're just tired out and try to wiggle your way out of card night. Think of the song "Butterfly Kisses" by Bob Carlisle and sing some of the words—that should put you on track. If that wouldn't work for you, come up with a stronger anchor. Let's go through a quick review: A.S.C.E.N.D.

1. Ascertain and specify your goals
2. Set goals in priority
3. Classify into short, medium, or long term
4. Establish action plan
5. Nail them down into daily tasks
6. Do it!

If you have any questions or get stuck, please e-mail me at dwrobel@wehelpyouachieve.com and I'll help you through it.

"Obstacles are things a person sees when he takes his eyes off his goals."
Eli Joseph Cossman

8

Partners, Mentors, and Coaches

This chapter covers the advantages of the unlimited knowledge and resources found in other people. First, here are some definitions from Dictionary.com: *partner*, one that is united with or associated with another in activity of common interest; *mentor*, a wise and trusted counselor; *coach*, a person who gives private instruction.

Let's talk about partners first. There are thousands of partners at the library—some dead some alive, it doesn't really matter. Since the first person created a pen and paper, people have been putting their thoughts, ideas, and knowledge on paper. We are fortunate enough to live in the age of technology when we are able to access thousands of books without ever leaving our house.

I love to go to the library or bookstore and to be surrounded by so many bright people with all of their ideas sitting on the shelves at my disposal. By tapping into the resources of other people's knowledge, you can accomplish almost anything you set goals for. If you are not utilizing the information that's available for your relationships or business, you really are not tapping all the potential for that area.

Abe Lincoln is one of my favorite partners. When I started reading books about him, I got a feeling about how he lived his life and made his decisions. During some rough times in my life, I tried to figure out how Honest Abe would handle the situation.

Your partners can be very much alive and present, too. They may be friends, associates, or people you meet at organized social events. Just bouncing ideas off someone who has a different perspective and a specific strength can open doors that never existed before.

The partnership is not based on compensation. The relationship is more of a discussion, getting advice from someone who is an expert or who has knowledge in a field that is not your strength. Partners can also have like-minded values and morals; then when you need a reality check, they are a great help in that area. Almost in the same way you set goals, decide which areas you need help in and find someone who has had a similar experience. You can benefit from their "been there, done that" Experience.

Take out your pen and paper and make a list of people you know, living or not, who have some talent or quality that you lack.. Then seek them out. Writing the list is the easy part; the hard part is deciding if their morals and values are in line with yours. This is important. If you bounce ideas and situations off people who are not in line with the way you live your life, it could lead to a difficult situation. So put some time into the investigative side of discovering who the person really is before you seek any ideas or suggestions. You'll find that when you approach people for help or a different perspective, they are often very open to the idea.

Having a mentor is very close to having a partner. The main difference is that a mentor is someone who really knows you and your values and is able to advise you on some of the tougher situations and decisions you will have to make in your life. In one sense, a mentor could almost be a grandfather figure, an old schoolteacher, an old coach; someone who will give you the truth even when you aren't willing to accept it. A mentor's advice is given with your and your family's best interest at heart because he or she has nothing to gain except to see you lead a happy and fulfilled life. The advice and insight from a mentor's life experiences is valuable. Don't overlook the fact that mentors are out there, even though no one has asked them to be mentors yet.

It's not necessary for mentors to be older. But I find the older they are, the more experience they've had. So they will have stories for almost any situation that I need advice on, and more likely than not, the advice would come from the journals of their own life. There is nothing better than getting firsthand advice. Okay, grab your pen and paper, and make a list of some people you know who really know you and what you're looking for in life. For some of you, it might be easy; for others, it might take a lot of work. Either way, it's worth the effort.

As with everything else, the first step is to write it down and then do it, follow through. Set a date that you will call them and then call. (Use Worksheet 13.) You don't want to turn it into a call-a-thon. Just ask them if from time to time you could give them a call for some sound advice. They will love it. If you're not sold on mentoring, you might try the relationship by volunteering to be a mentor to a child. You'll see the benefits both of you will realize from your relationship, and you will understand how the right mentor can significantly contribute to your life.

A coach is a mixture of a partner and a mentor. A coach will help you clarify some of your goals and discover your strengths. Through provocative questions, a coach will join you on your journey to self-discovery. He or she will help you set goals, hold you accountable, never judge you, be your cheerleader, and help you discover some of your hidden strengths. A coach is someone will direct all of his or her energies toward helping you achieve your objective.

The coaching industry has only been around for about ten years, but once it becomes part of the mainstream, everyone will have a coach. People hire personal trainers to help get physically fit. Well, a life coach does the same thing for your mind. There are coaches for executives, life, small businesses, and marriage. You name it, and there is a coach to fill that need. The good coaches always give a free session to help a potential client understand the benefits of their services. Once you see the results and how they get your brain moving, you will be hooked.

Having a coach is not about hype and excitement. That is just the end result of the sessions because you are able to see clearly your obstacles and goals. Coaches do not administer therapy or delve into your past and try to treat you. They simply help you plan your future in every part of your life that you choose. They motivate and encourage you, but they do not judge you. As a result, it's always a safe place to be able to get fresh ideas without someone putting limitations on you or reacting negatively. It's almost like having a positive self-talk outside your body. Coaches will not lie and give you false hope when there is none. If you are committed to having a more fulfilled life and you know there is more out there for you and you want more out of yourself and life, a coach is the answer.

Go to your computer, get on a search engine, and type in the kind of coach you would like information on. Tons of websites will pop up, so take your time and go through them. Take advantage of the free coaching sessions until you find the one who fits with who you are. Don't wait, time flies and waits for no one.

Make the decision that this year is your year to soar.

Partners/Mentors

Name	Relationship	Contact Information	Action Timetable

Worksheet 13

Conclusion

I have used and continue to use these skills in my life and business. I've also witnessed transformations in people's lives who used these simple skills and techniques. These skills were the most important ingredient in building my previous business and for my present business.

My goal for the reader is that they understand there *is* hope. Life *can* be better.

There is work involved, but the benefits are truly endless.

If you need direction or you're facing a crisis, midlife or just plain old life, you can find the necessary resources to overcome it and benefit by the experience. The resources will not come to you; you must go after them and not stop until you attain them. Cut out the negative things and people in your life; redesign your life balloon. It's never too late.

Remember the dreams you had when you were eighteen and full of hope and excitement? Just because you've lost those feelings along the way does not mean that you cannot find them again. Life goes by way too fast, and unfortunately, whether you decide to play or sit on the sidelines, time will continue to pass.

Once you begin your new journey in your brand-new balloon, you will start to see life from a whole different perspective, one of awe and amazement. Once you start dropping the sand bags that have weighed you down, you will soar! That is not even the exciting part; the exciting part is the people around you that will be influenced by your new life balloon. You will be an inspiration and model of what can be if you work at it.

Life will always throw trees and power lines in your route and sometimes a big gust of wind that you weren't counting on, but by having tremendous support from your basket and the good things you've been loading into your balloon, you will be able to spring right back on course. The important thing is to keep the sandbags from accumulating on your basket. When one appears, do what you have to do to cut it off. Your goal should always be to keep your balloon soaring. With persistence and clearly defined goals, there are no limits on how high you can go.

Get out that pen now and start today in designing your new life balloon. It does not matter where you are in life, at the very top or the very bottom. If you are not fulfilled, you must act now. You don't want to reach the end of your life filled with regret for all the things you wished you'd done. Start living today and soar in your new life balloon!

Notes

Notes

Notes

Notes

Notes

Notes

Notes

Notes

Notes

Notes

Notes

Notes

Notes

Notes

Notes

Notes

Notes

Notes

Notes

Notes

Notes

0-595-66225-0

Printed in the United States
17676LVS00001B/157-192